THE UNEXPLAINED

GHOSTS

AND THE
SUPERNATURAL

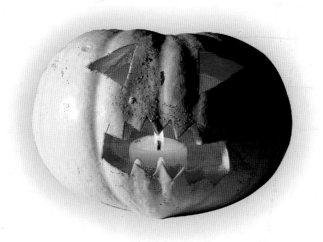

COLIN WILSON

DORLING KINDERSLEY
LONDON • NEW YORK • MOSCOW • SYDNEY

A DORLING KINDERSLEY BOOK

Project Editor *Amanda Rayner*

Art Editor *Alexandra Brown*

Managing Editor *Anna Kruger*

Managing Art Editor *Peter Bailey*

Picture Researcher *Tom Worsley*

Production *Ruth Cobb*

DTP Designer *Andrew O'Brien*

Designer *Robin Hunter*

First published in Great Britain 1998
by Dorling Kindersley Limited,
9 Henrietta Street, Covent Garden, London WC2 8PS

2 4 6 8 10 9 7 5 3 1

Copyright © 1998 Dorling Kindersley Ltd., London
Text copyright © Colin Wilson

Visit us on the World Wide Web at http://www.dk.com

A CIP catalogue record for this book is available from the British Library.

ISBN 0 7513 5682 4

Colour reproduction by G.R.B., Italy
Printed and bound by L.E.G.O., Italy

ACKNOWLEDGEMENTS

The Publisher would like to thank: Andy Crawford, Gary Ombler, and Sarah Ashun at DK Studios for specially commissioned photography; Mathew Birch and Robin Hunter for appearing as models; Catherine Edkins for additional picture research; and the following for their kind permission to reproduce their photographs:
(c=centre; b=bottom; l=left; r=right; t=top; a=above)

Adam Hart Davis: 8cl, 25tr; **AKG:** 9cl, 14clb, ca, 15cl, tr, 16c; **The Ancient Art & Architecture Collection Ltd:** 11tr; 14cr; **The Bridgeman Art Library:** 14c, 32tr; **The British Museum:** 35tc; **Dobson Agency:** 21crb; **Mary Evans Picture Library:** 9bc, 10cl, 11cb, bc

12cl, 13tl, 15cl, c, tl, cr, 17c, 18bl, 19br, 22clb, c, 23c, tl, 24tr, 27tc, tr, 28tr, clb, 29tl, 30crb, 31bc, 33c, 34bl, 35crb, 36tr, c, 37tl, cr; **Fortean Picture Library:** 4c, 7c, 8tl, bl, 9tr, 10cb, 13c, tr, 16tr, clb, 17tr, 18tr, 19tl, cra, 20cl, 23cr, 26tr, 27cr, crb, 28cb, 29tr, 31clb, tl, cr, 37c, tr; **Getty Images:** 25crb, 33tc; **The Ronald Grant Archive:** 13cr, 29c, 30tr, bl, 34cr; **Maurice Grosse:** 24cl; **The Hutchinson Library:** 32clb; **The Kobal Collection:** 26cr; **Simon Marsden:** 29cr; **Milepost 92½:** 18c; **Oxford Scientific Films:** 17cb, 23tr; **Rex Features:** 20c; **Frank Spooner Pictures:** 33tl; **Topham Picturepoint:** 12tr, 25tl; **Peter Underwood, President of the Ghost Club Society:** 26clb.

Jacket: **AKG:** front cb, back cra; **The Ancient Art & Architecture Collection Ltd:** back cra; **The Bridgeman Art Library:** back cra; **The British Museum:** inside back tr; **Mary Evans Picture Library:** inside front tl, back tl, back br, inside back br; **Fortean Picture Library:** front cl; c, cr; **The Ronald Grant Archive:** inside front bl; **Oxford Scientific Films:** front cl.

Every effort has been made to trace the copyright holders. Dorling Kindersley apologises for any unintentional omissions and would be pleased, in such circumstances, to add an acknowledgement in future editions.

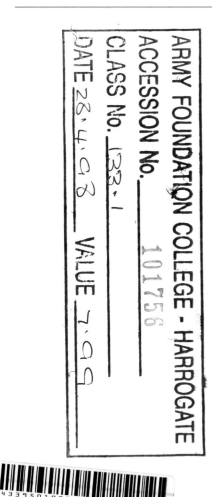

CONTENTS

INTRODUCTION

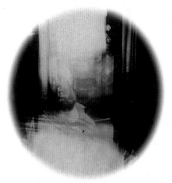

A ghostly figure that appeared on a television set in the USA

I have only once seen a ghost. I was sleeping in a haunted room in a house in Kensington Square, London, UK, and I woke up in the middle of the night to see a figure standing by my bed; it was shaped like a human, but seemed to be made of orange sparks. Strangely enough, I went back to sleep. To this day I have never known precisely what I saw.

Every civilisation in history has believed in life after death. All kinds of people accept that a ghost is the spirit of a dead person that remains on Earth, perhaps because it has some unfinished business or does not realize that it is dead, or possibly because the spirit was involved in some tragedy. Borley Rectory, in the UK, was apparently populated by several ghosts. Not all spirits are miserable – many people have seen friendly ghosts that haunt a particular place because it holds many happy memories for them.

Poltergeist activity in an Italian kitchen

Ghostly coach and horses

I have found that there are no hard-and-fast rules about ghosts. Some can only be seen by "sensitive" people, while others can only be captured on camera. Many apparitions are of people who have just died, who seem to want their relatives to know that they are dead. Other forms of ghostly activity seem to resemble "tape recordings" of tragic events that may be replayed over and over for centuries.

Poltergeists, or "noisy ghosts", are different from other phantoms because they play tricks on living people. In most cases, there is an unhappy teenager in the house and I am convinced that the spirit "steals" energy from young people to create mischief.

The Goatsucker from Puerto Rico

While ghosts are the best-known inhabitants of the supernatural world, there are many other weird creatures with evil reputations. Hundreds of eyewitness reports about vampires, werewolves, and the Goatsucker from Puerto Rico continue to mystify science.

Finally, many people claim to have seen another type of supernatural being – an angel that rescued them from harm. In other words, ghosts and supernatural beings are not necessarily frightening. They are simply baffling and, to people like me, extremely interesting.

Colin Wilson

A photograph that may show an angel

Borley Rectory – the most haunted house in the world?

TYPES OF GHOST

When most people imagine a ghost they picture a terrifying shape in flowing white robes. In fact ghosts look solid and normal and are often mistaken for real people. There are many different types of ghosts, including spirits that appear on the same day every year, ghosts that re-enact a specific event, uncanny "doubles", and even apparitions of living people.

CRISIS APPARITIONS

The most common type of ghost is the "crisis apparition". Thousands of people have seen an apparition of a close relative when the relative is on the point of death. Such ghosts may travel great distances and usually look solid. On 19th March 1917, Mrs Dorothy Spearman was feeding her baby in a hotel in Calcutta, India, when she realized that her half-brother was in the room. Then he vanished. Later she discovered that his plane had been shot down in Germany at the exact moment that he appeared to her.

Athenodorus sees a ghostly man in chains

A Classic Ghost Story

The familiar image of a restless spirit walking at night appears in the earliest known ghost story. In around 40 BC, the philosopher Athenodorus rented a haunted house in Athens, Greece. When he heard the sound of rattling chains and saw a sad old man, Athenodorus followed him into the garden. Suddenly the apparition vanished. The next day some workers dug at the spot and found a skeleton in rusty chains. When the bones were properly buried, the haunting ceased.

The cellar of the Treasurer's House, York, UK

Roman Tape Recording?

A "tape-recording" ghost is a replay of an event in the spirit's lifetime. These ghosts never react to human witnesses. In 1953, in the Treasurer's House, York, UK, Harry Martindale saw a legion of Roman soldiers, who were obviously unaware that he was there. As the ghosts marched along, the bottom half of their legs seemed to be under the floor. Perhaps their legs were partly hidden because the old Roman road was lower than the cellar floor.

" **Human personality** *does* **survive bodily death.** *"*

Professor H. Hart, Duke University, USA

The wife is alarmed by the sight of her husband, who is far away

The husband appears as a crisis apparition

Ghostly Anniversaries

Many ghosts appear every year on the same day and are known as "cyclic ghosts". The ghost of Anne Boleyn, the second wife of King Henry VIII of England, is seen on 24th December at her childhood home, Hever Castle, in Kent, UK. Anne was beheaded and according to legend she is seen with her head under her arm. Many ghosts appear on the anniversary of their death. An apparition resembling the film star Marilyn Monroe has been seen on 4th August, the day she died in 1962.

Hever Castle in Kent, UK

A shocked man sees his double

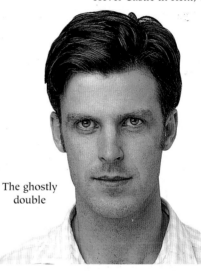

The ghostly double

Double Trouble

Many people have seen a ghostly "double" that looks exactly like them. The Empress Catherine of Russia saw her own double sitting on her throne, and ordered her guards to fire on it. In 1958, *Fate* magazine reported on a young man called Harold, who lived in Chicago, USA. He saw his own double whenever he had a bad migraine – it sat opposite him at the table and imitated every movement he made. The German word for this kind of double is "doppelgänger".

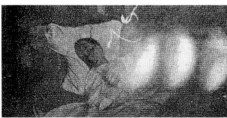

Nadine Baraduc 15 minutes after her death

The Departing Soul?

Many spiritualists believe that the soul leaves the body when a person dies and survives after death. For almost a century "spirit photographers" have tried to photograph the departing soul. Some images show a misty substance above the body of a dying person. In the image taken 15 minutes after Nadine Baraduc's death (above left) several "waves" of matter may be seen. It is possible that these waves are the soul of the Frenchwoman, who died in 1907.

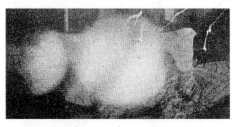

Nadine Baraduc one hour after her death

HAUNTED BUILDINGS

Most haunted houses have a tragic history. Borley Rectory, often called "the most haunted house in England", is haunted by the ghost of a nun who was murdered in the 17th century. Houses with a happy atmosphere are rarely haunted. However, a few do have a resident ghost – usually someone who was so attached to the house that they wanted to stay.

Sarah Winchester's house, San José, USA

Winchester House

Sarah Winchester, the last survivor of the famous Winchester family, moved into a farmhouse in San José, California, USA, i 1884. She believed that all the people wh had been killed by Winchester rifles had placed a curse on her family. Sarah received messages from her dead relative: telling her to add more and rooms to the house. They warned her that the curse would strike as soon she stopped buildin Sarah's ghost now haunts the corridors o the rambling mansion that she took 38 years to build.

BORLEY RECTORY

Borley Rectory, in Essex, UK, had several ghosts, including its first vicar, the Rev Henry Bull, who built the Rectory in 1863. Other spirits included a phantom nun and a ghostly coach that could be heard rattling up the drive. Many residents complained of poltergeists, including one vicar who was hit on the head with a hairbrush. After Borley Rectory mysteriously burned down in 1939, a woman's skull was found buried in its cellar. Could it have belonged to the phantom nun?

Borley Rectory,
Essex, UK

Haunted Churches

There are probably as many haunted churches as haunted houses. The ghosts are usually those of a priest or a monk kneeling at the altar. This well-known photograph (above) seems to show the ghost of a priest. It was taken in St Nicholas's Church in Arundel, Sussex, UK. Cameras often seem able to capture figures that are invisible to the eye, or which appear only as a faint blur of light.

House of Faces

In a house in Bélmez de la Moraleda, Spain, mysterious faces appear on the concrete kitchen floor. The first face appeared on 23rd August 1971. It was removed and the floor was laid with fresh cement. However, other faces immediately took its place – at one point there were no fewer than nine faces. The house had been built over a graveyard and ghost experts concluded that the faces were made by poltergeists. More recently the "House of Faces" has become a place of pilgrimage to those who believe that the faces are supernatural portraits of saints.

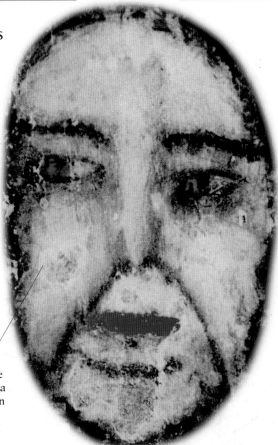

The expression seemed to change

Face on a concrete floor, Bélmez de la Moraleda, Spain

"I was glad to get away."

A visitor to Borley Rectory

The Raffles Hotel, Singapore

Raffles Hotel

The Raffles Hotel, one of the oldest hotels in Singapore, was haunted by the sound of a girl's voice singing an English nursery rhyme. The voice has been heard by hundreds of people. The hotel was built in 1897 on the site of a girls' boarding school, so the voice may be that of a long-dead pupil. The ghostly singer has not been heard since the old hotel was renovated in the 1980s. Her identity remains a mystery.

Amityville Hoax

The house in Amityville, Long Island, USA

A house in Amityville, Long Island was once the most famous haunted house in the USA. In 1974, Ronald DeFeo killed six members of his family there. In 1975, the Lutz family moved in but left after only a month. They claimed that they had been driven out by phantom footsteps, horrible smells, and ghostly hands. A book based on George Lutz's story, *The Amityville Horror*, became a best seller. However, the story proved to be a hoax. The family had left, unable to pay for the upkeep.

FAMOUS PHANTOMS

The ghosts of famous people seem to be particularly restless and there are many reported hauntings by kings and queens. Perhaps a forceful personality remains after death, causing their spirit to walk the Earth. Important events in a well-known person's life are sometimes re-enacted by apparitions in the places where they once lived or worked.

A HOST OF GHOSTS

The phantom forms of writers, politicians, emperors, and film stars have all been seen after their death. Some people think that ghosts meet other ghosts in the next world – imagine Abraham Lincoln talking to Queen Elizabeth I of England at a ghostly banquet. Some buildings seem to attract the spirits of famous people. Anne Boleyn (the second wife of King Henry VIII) and Sir Walter Raleigh both haunt the Tower of London, UK, the site of their execution.

Marilyn Monroe

Phantom Film Star

Marilyn Monroe was found dead on 4th August 1962. Some people believe that she died after taking too many sleeping pills but others think she was murdered. John Myers, a healer and psychic photographer, claims that Monroe's spirit told him that her death was an accident. Her ghost has been seen in a garden in Hollywood, USA, and a mirror once owned by the film star is said to be haunted by her image.

A group of famous ghosts

Ghost of Sir Walter Raleigh, seen at the Tower of London, UK

Ghost of Queen Elizabeth I, seen at Richmond Palace, UK

Ghost of Queen Anne Boleyn, beheaded in 1536

Napoleon Bonaparte inspecting his troops

Haunted by the President!

US president Abraham Lincoln was assassinated in 1865. His ghost has been seen by many people at the White House in Washington, DC. Soon after his death, a "spirit photographer" called William Mumler took this photograph (left) of a woman who came to see him. He was unaware that the woman was the wife of the murdered president. When it was developed, a spirit – thought to be Abraham Lincoln – could be seen behind her with his hands on her shoulders.

Mary Todd Lincoln with a ghostly figure

" The spirit of Lincoln still lives... "

F. D. Roosevelt, US president

Spectral Messenger

Napoleon Bonaparte died in exile on the island of St Helena in the Atlantic Ocean on 5th May 1821. On the same day, a stranger with his face muffled in his cloak arrived at Napoleon's mother's house in Rome, and insisted on seeing her. He told her that the Emperor had died that day. Then he hurried away. Madame Bonaparte asked which way the visitor had gone but her servant insisted that no one had left the house. Official news of her son's death did not reach Madame Bonaparte until 10 weeks later.

Ghost of Napoleon Bonaparte

Ghost of Queen Jane Seymour

Ghost of Abraham Lincoln

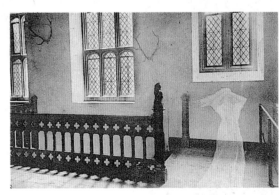
Hoax picture of Jane Seymour's ghost

Spirits of Queens

Ghosts of King Henry VIII's wives have been seen in several parts of the UK. Visitors to Hampton Court Palace near London have spotted an apparition that resembles Jane Seymour, who died in childbirth. Another of Henry's wives, Catherine Howard, was imprisoned in the Palace in 1541 but escaped from her guards, and ran to the chapel to beg the King for mercy. Henry ignored her, pretending to be at prayer. Catherine was dragged away shrieking and was executed soon afterwards. In recent times her terrible ghostly screams have echoed around the Palace.

PHANTOM ANIMALS

There are almost as many reports of phantom animals as of human ghosts. Pet owners are often aware that the spirits of dead pets are still around the house, apparently unwilling to leave their home. Although ghostly cats and dogs are most frequently reported, there have also been sightings of phantom horses, tigers, and other more unusual creatures.

GHOSTLY COACH AND HORSES

The sound of a spectral coach and horses was often heard outside Borley Rectory in Essex, UK. There have been many similar phantom coaches, including one that haunts Thorpe Hall, in Lincolnshire, UK, where two children claimed that they actually saw the coach. Since it is impossible for a coach to have a "spirit", many people believe that such phantoms are a kind of "tape recording" of a tragic event, which has somehow imprinted itself on a certain place.

Illustration of a black dog seen in 1577

Devilish Dogs

The folklore of many nations has tales of demonic black dogs – they are supposed to be the guardians of the underworld. The pamphlet shown above tells how, during a thunderstorm in 1577, a black dog appeared at the church in Bungay, Suffolk, UK, and ran down the aisle. Two people who were praying fell dead as it ran between them. Many country people believe that mischievous spirits like to take the form of black dogs.

A ghostly cat was seen at Killakee, Ireland, in 1968

Black Cat of Killakee

The Dower House in Killakee, Ireland, has a heavy front door that would not stay shut. Tom McAssey locked it but a strange voice said "Leave it open". McAssey fled in terror and looked back to see a large black cat with fiery eyes.

Ghostly horse-drawn
coaches are reported by
many witnesses

Apparitions of Pets

This photograph (right) of an Irish
wolfhound was taken in 1926. The
cairn puppy that appears behind it –
and which had been a special friend
of the wolfhound – had been dead
for six weeks. Many animals seem to
be unwilling to leave their human
owners. The medium Rosemary
Brown often saw phantom animals.
One night when her husband was ill,
and she was sitting beside him in
bed, she felt a weight on her legs,
and saw a tiger cub. When she
described the tiger to her
husband, he recognized it as
Sabrina, a pet owned by his
family in Egypt.

Photograph showing a ghostly puppy

Illustration from *The
Hound of the Baskervilles*

Hound of the Baskervilles

Sir Arthur Conan Doyle based his
Sherlock Holmes novel *The Hound
of the Baskervilles* on a true story.
In the 17th century, Richard
Cabell of Buckfastleigh, Devon,
UK, pursued his wife to the
nearby moor, and stabbed her to
death in a jealous rage. Her loyal
hound leapt for his throat and
killed him as he stabbed it. The
ghostly dog haunts the Cabell
family to this day.

Deadly Octopus

A vicar who moved into an old priory in
Wales, UK, woke up, freezing cold, in the
middle of a summer night. In the fireplace
he saw a writhing shape, like a slimy octopus
with pale, watery eyes. The monster seemed to
have paralysed him with a kind of will-force. He spent
the night praying and struggling to free himself. As morning
came, the creature finally disappeared and he never saw it again.

A monster in the shape
of an octopus tried to
kill a British man

A LIFE OF THEIR OWN

Can ships and trains turn into ghosts? Can objects like clocks and cars be haunted? Incredible though it may seem, such things can really happen. Some objects appear to have a life of their own, while others may have supernatural powers. There have been many explanations for such ghostly activity – from poltergeists to curses – but none really provides a satisfactory answer.

LINCOLN'S PHANTOM TRAIN

The ghost of US president Abraham Lincoln, who was murdered in 1865, has been sighted many times in the White House, in Washington, DC. It is also said that the train used to take his body from Washington, DC to Illinois still haunts the Albany railway line. For many years the train was seen at midnight on 27th April, the anniversary of the journey. Witnesses claim that the air becomes strangely still before the ghostly black train rushes past in total silence, with black flags flying, and a crew of phantoms.

Models of the heads found in
Hexham, Northumberland, UK, in 1972

Cursed Heads?

In 1972, Colin and Leslie Robson found two carved heads the size of tennis balls in their garden at Hexham, near Newcastle, UK. Indoors the heads moved by themselves and crockery was smashed. Historian Anne Ross thought the heads were Celtic and about 1,800 years old. A previous tenant of the Hexham house claimed that he had made the heads for his children, but when Dr Ross took them home she saw a "wolf man" and quickly got rid of them.

US president
Abraham Lincoln's
funeral train

The *Flying Dutchman* "ghost ship"

The *Flying Dutchman*

Many sailors claim to have seen the "ghost ship" known as the *Flying Dutchman*. According to legend, its captain was a Dutchman, Hendrik Van der Decken. The captain shouted such fearful curses as he sailed around the Cape of Good Hope in a storm, that some supernatural force condemned him to sail the seas for eternity. Sightings of the *Flying Dutchman* are rumoured to bring bad luck, often death. On 11th July 1881, Britain's future king, George V, saw the ship in Australian waters. Fortunately, he escaped its bad luck – he died at the mature age of 70.

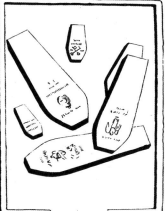

Coffins in the Chase family
tomb before...

... and after their last
disturbance, in 1820

The Moving Coffins

For more than eight years, a mysterious force moved the coffins in a sealed tomb on the island of Barbados in the West Indies. The strange events began in 1812 when the tomb was opened to bury a member of the Chase family. The coffins were found overturned, although the tomb had been sealed. The coffins were duly rearranged and the tomb was tightly sealed again. However, in the following years, every time the tomb was opened to bury someone, it was found in disorder. In 1820, the Governor of Barbados ordered the coffins to be removed and the tomb has since remained empty. No explanation has ever been found.

A small boy in
the passenger seat

Photograph apparently showing a boy's head inside a car

Is This Car Haunted?

No one can explain why there should be a small boy's head inside this car, photographed in Bradley, West Yorkshire, UK, in March 1974. When the photograph was taken, the car appeared to be empty. Perhaps the head belongs to the ghost of a golden-haired boy who is sitting in the passenger seat. Or is the image just a trick of the light?

The Stopped Clock

There are many stories of grandfather clocks stopping at the moment of the owner's death. A man called Stephen died in Winnipeg, Canada, at the age of 72. After his death the clock would have passed to the male heir but Stephen only had daughters. A year later the clock started up again at the moment when his youngest daughter gave birth to a son. The son would eventually inherit his grandfather's clock and it may have started to celebrate his birth.

Grandfather clock

Clouds cover the Moon as the phantom rain goes by."

Extract from the
Albany Times

IN TUNE WITH GHOSTS

One of the strangest things about ghosts is that many people would not notice if one was standing right beside them. Out of a dozen people in a haunted room, only two might see the ghost. It seems that someone's mind must be "tuned in" to see a spirit, just like tuning in a television set, and not everyone can do this.

THE MAN IN GREY

The Theatre Royal in Drury Lane, London, UK, has one of the world's best-known ghosts – the "Man in Grey". Many actors have seen him, indeed actors seem particularly sensitive to ghosts. The "Man in Grey" wears old-fashioned clothes and walks along the aisle in the upper circle. The identity of the restless spirit remains puzzling, although it may belong to the man whose skeleton was discovered in the theatre in 1848 with a dagger between his ribs.

Possible photograph of a ghost

"Old Nanna's Here!"

Children are often more sensitive to ghosts than adults, and there are hundreds of cases of children seeing dead relatives. This photograph was taken in 1991, after a two-year-old boy said, "Old Nanna's here," and pointed into the air. The whitish shape may be the ghost of the boy's great-grandmother.

Computer reconstruction of the "Man in Grey"

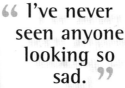

" I've never
seen anyone
looking so
sad. "

W. Macqueen Pope
on seeing the
"Man in Grey"

Falling painting

The Ghost that Moved Pictures

When Frances Freeborn moved into a house in
Bakersfield, California, USA, in 1981, she did not
expect to encounter the spirit of the previous owner.
The spirit seemed to disapprove of her alterations to
the house and when Frances tried to hang an old
picture in several different places, it was always on
the floor the next morning. Then she felt directed
to hang it in a bedroom. When she had done so it
stayed on the wall. Frances felt that the picture was
too low but it seemed just right for the spirit, who
had been a very short woman.

An image from Annie Smith's cine film, 1972

Ghosts of the Living

Mrs Annie Smith from Yorkshire, UK, was
involved in a frightening road accident in
1972 when a truck pulled out in front of her
car. There was a terrible collision that left Annie
and her husband badly shaken but unhurt. This
photograph (above) is part of Annie's film taken
just after the accident for insurance purposes.
Who is the person sitting in her seat? Psychic
investigators believe it is a "crisis image" of
Annie, imprinted on the film by her fear.

SPIRIT MESSAGES

Spiritualists believe that everyone can communicate with the dead. They are convinced that people who have died continue to exist after they have "passed over to the other side". People who talk to the dead are called "mediums". Many mediums, or psychics, go into a trance to receive spirit messages. Occasionally, even people with no psychic gifts receive unexpected news from the other world.

ECTOPLASM FROM HER NOSE!

Some mediums produce ectoplasm from their nose or mouth when they are in a trance. It is a substance that looks like a delicate fabric but it seems to be made of a material similar to the white of an egg. Sometimes ectoplasm shapes itself into human faces, hands, or even bodies. This photograph (right) shows Margery Crandon, an American medium, producing ectoplasm from her nose.

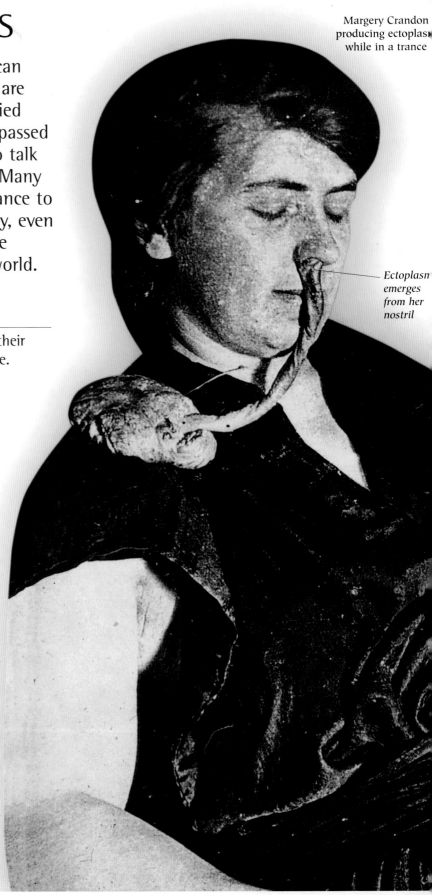

Margery Crandon producing ectoplasm while in a trance

Ectoplasm emerges from her nostril

A spirit made of ectoplasm taking shape

Materialized Spirit
The photograph above shows a spirit made of ectoplasm. The 19th-century "spirit guide" John King explained that he took ectoplasm from the brain of the medium, and from the brains of people sitting nearby. Then he moulded it, as a sculptor moulds clay, into the face and body of a spirit who had communicated with him.

Marianne

I CANNOT UNDERSTAND
TELL ME MORE

Marianne,

STILL CANNOT UNDERSTAND
PLEASE TELL ME MORE

Mysterious writing at Borley Rectory, UK

The Writing on the Wall

The unreadable words (above), written on a wall at Borley Rectory, UK, were addressed to the vicar's wife Marianne Foyster. They seem to be an attempt by a spirit to communicate, though Marianne explained in block capitals that she could not understand. The British psychic Matthew Manning has also discovered "spirit writing". The walls of his house have been covered with more than 300 signatures as well as messages in Arabic and Russian.

> ## " I am sure her trance was genuine. "
>
> US psychologist William James on the medium Leonora Piper, 1885

Photograph of a girl with the spirit of her dead sister

Spirit Photographs

A mysterious figure is occasionally captured on film. Often the person in the photograph recognizes the form as a dead relative; sometimes the apparitions are completely unknown. In 1973, Stella Lansing, a US psychic, was shocked to discover a turbaned man with a flute on film she had taken with her cine camera. The film should have shown her favourite television programme.

Winged Messengers

Many families have experienced a ghostly white bird that appears to foretell death. When Mother Oxenham, the head of a family from Devon, UK, lay dying in 1618, a white bird was seen in her bedroom. It appeared many years later to foretell the death of her grandson, and has been appearing ever since when a member of the family is near death. The Arundel family from Wiltshire, UK, usually sees two ghostly white owls just before the death of a relative.

A white bird is believed to be an omen of death

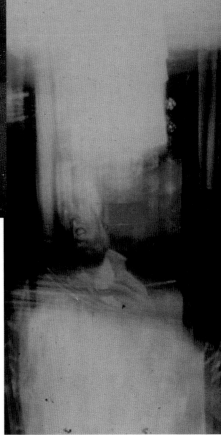

A still from Stella Lansing's film shows a ghostly man on her television screen

POLTERGEISTS

Poltergeists, or "noisy spirits", make loud noises, cause objects to fly across rooms, and even start fires. They usually haunt families with children or teenagers. Some experts think that poltergeists are caused by the unconscious minds of unhappy young people. Others believe they are ghosts trapped on Earth who "steal" their energy from disturbed teenagers.

The Amherst house, USA, in 1878

MISCHIEF-MAKERS

Although poltergeists often throw heavy objects with great force, it is rare for them to actually hurt anybody. In one case, a huge potato flew across the room, narrowly missing someone's head, and shattered into pieces against the wall. In another, a heavy silver teapot was hurled through the air, but turned at right angles before it struck anyone, as if the poltergeist was holding it rather than throwing it. Poltergeists can even make objects go through walls, for which there is no scientific explanation.

The Amherst Mystery
When 18-year-old Esther Cox from Amherst, Nova Scotia, USA, split up with her boyfriend she was tormented by a ghost. The spirit wrote on her bedroom wall "Esther, you are mine to kill", pulled the sheets off her bed, and made her body swell like a balloon. When Esther took a job in a restaurant, fires broke out and knives and forks stuck to her as if she were a magnet. Accused of causing the fires, she was sent to prison where the disturbances stopped.

Janet Harper from Enfield, UK, apparently levitating

Levitating Spirit
In 1977, the Harper family from Enfield, UK, experienced strange disturbances. Furniture moved on its own and objects flew through the air. Investigators Guy Playfair and Maurice Grosse photographed 11-year-old Janet Harper floating in mid-air while asleep. A Dutch medium, Dono Gmelig-Meyling, declared that the house seemed to be full of spirits from the local graveyard. He somehow persuaded them to go away.

Poltergeist activity – objects flying through the air

A telephone flies past a 14-year-old girl

Flying Pots and Pans
Most poltergeist disturbances are reasonably short-lived, lasting about two months. In that time, every room in a house may be turned upside down. This photograph (right) of flying kitchen utensils is typical of poltergeist activity. It was taken in the home of the Costa family from St Jeanne de Maurienne, Italy, in June 1955. Teresa Costa was the "focus" – that is, the poltergeist "stole" her energy to cause chaos.

Teresa Costa and her baby watching strange events in their kitchen

Telephone Terror
This photograph (above) shows a telephone flying across the lap of a 14-year-old girl called Tina. On 4th March 1984, her family were driven to leave their home in Columbus, Ohio, USA, by a poltergeist that threw things, switched lights on and off, and turned on the shower. A reporter named Fred Shannon came to see the family and snapped this photograph, which appeared in a local newspaper.

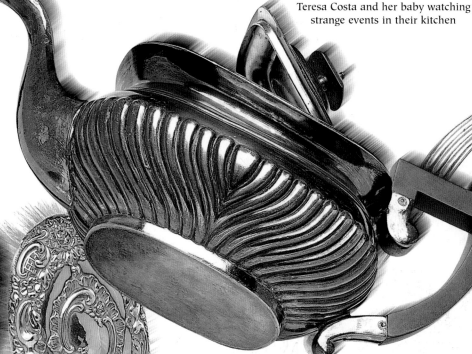

Sandringham House, Norfolk, UK

Royal Uproar
Sandringham House in Norfolk, UK, a residence of the British royal family, plays host to a poltergeist on 24th December every year. Sheets are stripped off freshly made beds and Christmas cards are thrown on the floor. The sound of heavy breathing is heard from a room off the footman's corridor. One footman refused to sleep there after he saw something that resembled "a large paper sack breathing in and out like a grotesque lung".

THE GHOST HUNTERS

If you think you have a ghost in your home, you can call in an expert to investigate. Many ghost hunters use special equipment to find out whether hauntings are real or just hoaxes. Although many spirits are not visible to the naked eye, strange apparitions have been caught on camera. Far from being rare, ghosts seem almost as common as cats and dogs.

GHOSTBUSTING IN THE MOVIES

In the film *Ghostbusters* (1984) a team of ghost hunters used special laser guns to rescue New York from a plague of spirits. Various characters called in the exterminating team with hilarious results. However, the events shown in the movie do not match real-life investigations. Most psychic researchers use sophisticated equipment to collect data and do not attempt to remove any ghost from its home.

The famous ghost hunter, Harry Price

Real-life Ghost Hunter

Harry Price was a British magician who used his knowledge of tricks to investigate hauntings, and to decide whether they could be hoaxes. Price soon realized that ghosts really exist, and during the 1930s he became the most famous ghost hunter in the world. He also uncovered several hoaxes by lonely people who had "manufactured" a ghost to keep them company.

Camera

Powerful light

A case for transporting equipment

Torch

Notebook

Magnifying glass

Tape recorder

Ghost-hunting equipment used by Peter Underwood, President of the Ghost Club Society, UK

Ghost-detecting Equipment

Certain equipment is very useful for investigating haunted houses: a camera with infra-red film (to take photographs in the dark), an ordinary camera with a flash unit, a powerful light, a tape recorder, and a thermometer (ghosts cause a room to go cold). Finally, talcum powder scattered on the floor will record footprints.

A still from the film *Ghostbusters* (1984)

Hoax Photograph

Ghost experts never take anything for granted and many photographs have turned out to be hoaxes. The image on the right was taken in 1891 as Lord Combermere from Cheshire, UK, was being buried. The figure in the armchair is believed to be his spirit but the photograph may be a fake. In 1895 two men set out to create a hoax image of a ghost (far right) using special photography. The shadowy form strongly resembles the ghost of Lord Combermere in the earlier photograph.

Sybell Corbet's photograph of the library at Combermere, Cheshire, UK, 1891

Hoax photograph taken by Professor Barrett and Gordon Salt in 1895

The Brown Lady

Raynham Hall in Norfolk, UK, is haunted by a "Brown Lady" ghost. The Victorian novelist Captain Marryat saw her one night in 1835 when he was returning to his room and fired his pistol at her. The lady glared at him and vanished. In 1936, a photographer for a British magazine recorded the apparition on film. His assistant saw a shadowy figure on the stairs, but the photographer saw nothing. When the film was developed, a strange figure appeared (right).

Photograph taken at Raynham Hall

The churchyard at Prestbury, Gloucestershire, UK

Graveyard Ghost

An abbot dressed in black is supposed to haunt the churchyard at Prestbury, Gloucestershire, UK. A photographer called Derek Stafford visited the floodlit graveyard on 22nd November 1990 in an attempt to photograph the "Black Abbot". In his photograph a supernatural shadow seems to be looming over the graves.

BLOODSUCKERS

According to legend, a vampire can live forever – provided that he or she can stay alive by drinking the blood of the living. Anyone bitten by a vampire also turns into a vampire. Most vampires are male and fly by turning themselves into bats. Recent reports from Puerto Rico of a weird blood-sucking creature suggest that vampires may still be at large in the world.

Elisabeth Bathory

VAMPIRES

There is a disturbing amount of solid evidence for real-life vampires – blood-sucking human beings like the fictional Dracula. In the first famous case, in 1732, the villagers of Medvegia, in Serbia, complained that vampires were walking at night. Emperor Charles VI of Austria ordered the opening of a dozen graves and all the bodies looked as fresh as when they were buried. The bodies were all burnt, and their ashes thrown in the river. Medvegia was never troubled with vampires again.

Bathory's Blood Baths
Elisabeth Bathory was a wealthy Hungarian countess who lived in the 17th century. She believed that drinking and bathing in human blood would keep her young. Bathory ordered the death of dozens of her servant girls and drained their blood for her gruesome beauty treatments. Eventually she was walled up in her own room and left to die.

A vampire from a modern film

Prince Vlad V of Wallachia

The Castle of Bran, once the home of Prince Vlad, Transylvania, Romania

The Real Dracula
Prince Vlad V of Wallachia (now part of Romania) was also known as "Dracul" (the devil). He was the inspiration for Bram Stoker's novel *Dracula* and a brutal tyrant who loved to impale living people on stakes. It is said that he feasted on human flesh and the blood of his enemies. Vlad was finally killed in battle, possibly by his own men, in 1477.

Driving a stake into a vampire's grave

Killing a Vampire

According to ancient tradition, a vampire can only be killed by having a stake driven through his heart. However, in many Mediterranean countries, the corpse of a suspected vampire (which is easy to recognize because the body looks so fresh in the grave) was always burned, and the ashes scattered into a river or the sea.

Artist's impression of the Goatsucker

Grisly Goatsucker

On the Caribbean island of Puerto Rico, a strange monster known as the Goatsucker has been killing chickens, rabbits, goats, and even cows, throughout the 1990s. The animals are left drained of blood and with organs missing. Witnesses say that the creature has large fangs, glowing eyes, pointed ears, and claw-like hands.

The Dracula Society

Graves at St Mary's Church, Whitby, Yorkshire, UK

Graveyards have always been popular settings for spine-chilling tales – for example, the graves at St Mary's Church in Whitby, Yorkshire, UK, featured in Bram Stoker's novel, *Dracula*. The graveyard was chosen by Count Dracula for his first attack in Britain. In modern times, members of the Dracula Society meet in Whitby every summer. They wear white, death-mask make-up and black cloaks in honour of the legendary count.

CREATURES OF THE NIGHT

Many people have reported seeing weird creatures like werewolves, the Jersey devil, and the Dover demon. These beasts all seem to have supernatual powers and hide under cover of darkness. This has led some groups to suggest that they are visitors from other worlds. Although these monsters sound too bizarre to be real, eyewitness reports are full of convincing details.

A still from the film *I Was A Teen-age Werewolf*

WEREWOLVES

A werewolf is a man who is supposed to change into a wolf every month at the full Moon. In medieval times when wolves were common in Europe and greatly feared as evil creatures, there were many werewolf legends. Werewolf stories have persisted in modern times. In 1975, a British teenager committed suicide because he was convinced he was turning into a wolf. Legend has it that a werewolf can only be killed by a silver bullet.

A werewolf transformed by the full Moon

Monsters at the Movies
In early werewolf films the tragic hero is doomed to change into a murderous beast whenever there is a full Moon. Later films, like *I Was A Teen-age Werewolf* (1957), use grisly "special effects" to show the man's transformation into a hideous monster.

A werewolf returning home

True Stories
Some people have truly believed that they were werewolves. Gilles Garnier was executed in France in 1574 for attacking children. He said he had become a wolf at the time of the attacks. Peter Stubbe from Germany was sentenced to death in 1587 when he confessed to many killings after changing into a wolf.

I Saw the Dover Demon!

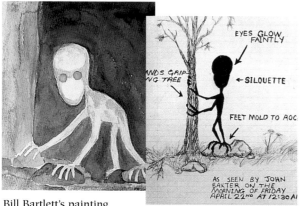

Bill Bartlett's painting
of the strange creature

John Baxter's sketch seems to
show the same mysterious beast

A creature with a huge head, a tiny body, and slender fingers was seen by several young people on 21st and 22nd April 1977. When 15-year-old John Baxter spotted the creature in Dover, near Boston, USA, it seemed very frightened and ran away. Another witness, Bill Bartlett, aged 17, painted a picture of the strange being. A group of flying-saucer investigators thought that it might be an alien from a spaceship and experts who interviewed the boys believed their stories. Local newspaper reports coined a nickname for the creature – "the Dover demon".

Spring-heeled Jack

In 1838, London, UK, was terrorized by a strange figure in a huge cloak with claw-like hands and fiery red eyes. When pursued, the creature bounded away over walls. Spring-heeled Jack, as it was called, attacked dozens of people but no one could catch the monster, who stalked the streets at night and jumped like a kangaroo.

19th-century image of
Spring-heeled Jack

The Beast of Gévaudan

Between 1764 and 1767, a wolf as big as a donkey killed more than 60 people in the Gévaudan region of France. Eventually several hundred trackers set out to kill it. The man who finally shot the monstrous beast in the heart used a silver bullet to ensure its certain death. The wolf's body was paraded through the region for more than a week to reassure everyone that it was really dead.

Hunting the Beast of Gévaudan

Jersey Devil

In January 1909, people in New Jersey, USA, were terrified by a creature with a horse's head and bat-like wings, which left strange tracks in the snow. On one occasion, the monster swooped down on a group of fire-fighters who fled in terror. After a few weeks, the sightings stopped and its identity remains a mystery to this day.

Sketch of the Jersey devil based on
eyewitness descriptions

Huge, leathery
wings like a
giant bat's

Cloven hoofs

GHOSTLY FESTIVALS

In Europe and the United States you often hear the question: "Do you believe in ghosts?" In other parts of the world such as Mexico and Japan, ghosts are included in family celebrations. People believe that the dead rejoin their relatives in eating, drinking, and having fun. They are not lost to the living and can still enjoy themselves.

HALLOWE'EN

Hallowe'en on 31st October is really a ghost festival. It was originally an ancient Celtic ritual in which the souls of the dead were believed to revisit their homes, and fires were lit to drive away evil spirits, hobgoblins, and demons. Under Christianity it was known as All Saints' Day, or Hallowed Evening (which became Hallowe'en). Today, children celebrate by making spooky pumpkins. They wear frightening masks and knock on doors demanding "Trick or treat".

Japanese painting of a spirit with a ghostly lantern

Feast of Lanterns

The Japanese Feast of Lanterns (13th–15th July) is also a ghost festival. People offer food to their dead relatives and tea is poured for the invisible guests every hour. At night, homes are decorated with beautiful lanterns fringed with paper streamers. Virtually all Japanese people believe in ghosts, and care for their dead relatives at this special time as if they were alive.

Dogon dancers, Mali, Africa

Dogon Mourning Rites

The Dogon people from Mali, in West Africa, are ancestor worshippers. When a member of the tribe dies, the men mark the end of mourning with a "dama" – a rite that aims to settle the troubled souls of the dead and send them safely on their way to the afterlife. Dancers wear a variety of striking masks and perform elaborate dances, mock battles, and rites that can last up to six days, depending on the importance of the dead person.

Hallowe'en pumpkin

The Mexican Day of the Dead festival

The Day of the Dead

On 2nd November, Mexico's Day of the Dead, the dead revisit the living, and it is a time of great joy as well as sadness. Families prepare food, drink, and flowers and the offerings are left on a candle-lit table for the dead to enjoy. Men dressed as devils or skeletons dance in the streets and children eat sweets in the shape of skulls. On the following night, families go to the cemetery and sit with lighted candles talking about their dead relatives.

Grim Reaper model from the Day of the Dead festival

A wand used in the Ghost Dance

Illustration of a native North American Ghost Dance

Dancing with Ghosts

By 1870, many native North Americans were half-starved because white people had killed so many buffalo. They performed the Ghost Dance, a magic ceremony to make the white people go away. Dancers had visions in which they visited the spirit world and met dead relatives. At first the Ghost Dance seemed to work and white soldiers were forced to retreat. However, on 23rd December 1890, US troops massacred 200 men, women, and children at Wounded Knee in South Dakota and the days of the Ghost Dance were over.

SPELLS AND SORCERY

Charms and magic spells are used by many people to protect themselves against evil. They are necessary because in some parts of the world voodoo sorcerers are greatly feared. These individuals have the power to create zombies or the "living dead". Evil spirits are very real for some people and special ceremonies are held to scare them away.

ZOMBIES

Voodoo is a religious cult involving witchcraft, that is practised in the West Indies. Many West Indian people believe in zombies, or "the walking dead". A ghost is a spirit without a body but a zombie is the opposite – a body without a spirit. Voodoo sorcerers may use certain quick-acting poisons, like that from the puffer fish, to put a person into a death-like state. After burial, a victim is dug up by the sorcerer who poisoned him or her, drugged, and forced to work as a slave.

Four-leaf clover

Horseshoe

Little Buddha

Lucky Charms

Many people carry tiny Buddhas and four-leaf clovers to bring them good luck. Other charms such as horseshoes are believed to make the owner lucky in love or business. Do these charms really work? They can certainly make you feel lucky and most people have noticed that when they feel lucky they are lucky.

> **" that blank face with the dead eyes... "**
> Zora Hurston speaking about a real-life zombie

The Living Dead

In October 1936, a woman was found in Haiti wandering around in a daze. Her father recognized her as Felicia Felix-Mentor, who had died of a fever in 1907 and been buried. It seems that she had worked as a slave for her voodoo master for almost 30 years before finally escaping. An American scientist named Zora Hurston who studied Felicia noticed the dreadful blankness of her eyes – although Felicia was alive, she seemed numb to everything around her.

Felicia Felix-Mentor, a zombie found in 1936

A Hollywood image of a zombie

Eye of Horus

Carved wooden head from West Africa

Scaring Away Evil

The amulet or lucky charm shown above comes from ancient Egypt, and was placed on mummified bodies to protect them. The eye belongs to the god Horus and had the power to heal. Charms are still used in the 20th century to cure sickness and keep away evil – many are made by African witch doctors. This carving of a woman's head (right) was left at the entrance of a village to scare off evil spirits. Terrifying masks are worn in the secret ceremonies of the Ibibio people to ward off evil.

Japanese exorcism, 19th-century illustration

Exorcising Evil Spirits

Can evil spirits get inside us and make us do things we do not want to do? In Japan, people believe that animal spirits can possess human beings. Many religions believe in possession, and they have special rituals and prayers that are intended to drive out the evil spirit. The ceremony is called "exorcism". In most countries the exorcist is a priest or a witch doctor who uses powerful magic. The priest addresses the spirit directly and commands it to leave its victim.

HEAVENLY WONDERS

Extraordinary events and fantastic visions happen every day somewhere in the world. As the 20th century nears its end these enigmas continue to baffle the experts. Glowing lights in the sky, miraculous cures for severe illnesses, and visitations by angels seem to defy the laws of science. The supernatural world is very much alive and well.

Pilgrims at Lourdes, France

VISIONS IN THE SKY

On 13th May 1917, near Fatima, Portugal, three children saw the shining figure of a woman above a tree. She told them she was from heaven, and would appear on the same day every month for six months. Many people came to the spot, but only the children could see her. Finally, on 13th October 1917, when thousands of people had gathered in heavy rain, a bright disc descended from the sky. When the light vanished the people were astonished to find that their clothes were completely dry.

Miracle Cures

On 11th February 1858, a 14-year-old girl called Bernadette Soubirous saw a vision of a woman in white outside a cave in Lourdes, France. The woman told her to dig in the cave, and a spring bubbled up. The waters of this spring are said to possess healing powers. Every year, sick people from all corners of the world go on a pilgrimage to Lourdes and many go home cured. Believers have no doubt that the vision was the Virgin Mary.

INDEX

Angels on a stained glass window

Messengers from Above

"Angel" is a Hebrew word meaning messenger. In the Bible, angels are the messengers of God who bring people good news and come to help them. Many people have felt protected by a "guardian angel". In 1985, an American named Shari Peterson was involved in a plane crash. She believes that an angelic voice saved her life by telling her to fasten her seat belt only seconds before part of the aircraft blew away.

A Modern Marvel?

On the day after his mother died in 1978, a Swiss man named Silvio took this photograph (above) of a ball of light. When developed, the photograph revealed an unusual shape. Was it the spirit of Silvio's mother? Or some kind of energy, shaped into a human figure by the power of Silvio's mind? Or could it have been an angel sent to give him comfort?

"The light was dancing in the sky."

An eyewitness from Fatima, Portugal

Pilgrims watch the vision near Fatima, Portugal

Photograph taken in a Hungarian church

Apparition of Mary and Jesus?

On 3rd September 1989, Károly Ligeti asked a man to take a photograph of him in the church at Karácsond, Hungary. This picture (above) was taken as Ligeti suddenly saw a female figure surrounded by light, with her hand on the shoulder of a child. Could it have been the Virgin Mary and Jesus?

Angels of Mons

Illustration of the angels of Mons

On 29th September 1914, a British newspaper published a story by Arthur Machen, which claimed that phantom bowmen had appeared in the sky at the battle of Mons, in France. In the story, German soldiers ran for their lives at the sight of these "angels". When British troops finally returned from Mons, many claimed that they really had seen the angels. Machen insisted that he made up the story but the soldiers gave detailed accounts of their heavenly visitors.